Blessings to you
as you read and
study God's word.
Kay Kevan Callentine
Psalm
121

Between God and Me

KAY KEVAN CALLENTINE

WESTBOW
PRESS®
A DIVISION OF THOMAS NELSON
& ZONDERVAN

WestBow Press books may be ordered through booksellers or by contacting:

WestBow Press
A Division of Thomas Nelson & Zondervan
1663 Liberty Drive
Bloomington, IN 47403
www.westbowpress.com
1 (866) 928-1240

ISBN: 978-1-5127-2772-2 (sc)
ISBN: 978-1-5127-2771-5 (e)

Library of Congress Control Number: 2016900964

Print information available on the last page.

WestBow Press rev. date: 1/22/2016

Dedicated to my husband Jim

March 19, 1948-February 11, 2015

You Have Been Redeemed

Satan leads us into sinful paths;
Jesus offers green pastures.
Satan speaks in cunning lies;
Jesus expresses only Truth.

Satan wants you to be condemned;
Jesus says you are forgiven.
Satan will take you to hell;
Jesus provides the Way to heaven.

Satan wants you to die;
Jesus gives you life in Him.
Satan leaves you stranded and alone;
Jesus provides you with His armor.

The wiles of the devil
Lead to destruction and death.
The ways of the Lord
Grant resurrection with Christ.

Following Satan offers no peace;
Accepting the Savior brings joy.
The devil wants you to wallow in despair;
God declares Remember Me.

"Remember that the Lᴏʀᴅ rescued you…in order to make you his very own people and his special possession, which is what you are today." Deuteronomy 4:20 (NLT)

Scriptures to enjoy:

Psalm 23:2
John 14: 6
John 11:25-26
Ephesians 6:10-17
Deuteronomy 4:20

Prayer: Jesus, You are the Way to heaven and the only Hope for today. Thank You for Your saving grace. In Your Name I pray. Amen.

You are Set Free

Have you ever felt like you were in bondage to something? It could have been a bad habit or addiction, a debt or unwanted obligation, or some other restraint that held you captive. Then have you ever felt the exhilaration of being set from that bondage? Or does it still have strings to which you are attached?

The hold of Satan on our lives is real and it is strong. It is only through the power of Christ that we can be set free from whatever control the devil has on us, whether addiction or habit or lifestyle that is not what God wants for us. If we don't know Jesus as Lord and Savior, the control Satan has over us will not be loosed.

Praise God! He has set us free and broken the hold sin has over us. When we accept Him, He sets us free from whatever has held us captive; the bondage of sin and destruction is gone. The change may be immediate in our lives or it may take hold gradually as we grow in our faith and relationship with the Lord. But once we surrender our lives to the Lord Jesus Christ and name Him as Savior for our lives He is now in control of us through the Holy Spirit. And that power is greater than all our sin and any other thing that we have been in captivity to. Jesus gives us new life in Him. He calls us in scripture a "new creation." "This means that anyone who belongs to Christ has become a new person. The old life is gone; a new life has begun!" 2 Corinthians 5:17 (NLT) He shows us the way to heaven. "Jesus told him, "I am the way, the truth, and the life. No one can come to the Father except through me."" John 14:6 (NLT)

Scriptures to enjoy:

Galatians 4:5-7
Galatians 3:21-23
Galatians 5:1-13
John 14:6

Prayer: Thank You, Jesus, for setting me free from my bondage. I pray others will find this freedom as well. In Your name I pray. Amen.

Wow Moments

Imagine Moses's experience standing at the burning bush and not seeing it consumed. That must have been a "wow" moment for him. Or the time the Israelites observed that smoke wrapped Mt. Sinai as the Lord's presence descended and He spoke in the thunder as He called Moses up to Him. Another "wow" for Moses no doubt. Then there were the shepherds who heard the angels sing announcing the birth of Jesus. What an experience that would have been! Think of the moments of your life that heralded events to be remembered: your marriage, the birth of your child, the prized award you earned in your career. What was your "wow" moment?

Do we celebrate "wow" moments with Jesus in our lives? Do you realize that when you accepted Jesus you started your journey to heaven? We travel now by faith but we will see Jesus face to face. What a day to remember that will be. In the meantime, create "wow" moments as you share that growing relationship with your Savior.

Scriptures to enjoy:
Exodus 3:1-2
Exodus 19:18-20
1 Corinthians 13:12

Prayer: Jesus, thank You for the events in our lives that You give us to cherish. Help us to grow daily in our love for others and in our relationship with You as You prepare us on our journey to heaven. Amen.

When is the right time to give your life to Jesus?

Are you waiting for a more convenient time? What if this was your last moment in this life? Your opportunity to say yes to Jesus would be gone and you would face an eternal separation from Christ in hell. You wouldn't have a more convenient time. You are guaranteed only this moment in your life. The past is gone forever and a future on this earth may not come for you. Make the decision to accept Jesus as your Savior now. "Now is the day of salvation." 2 Corinthians 6:2 (NKJV) There won't ever be a more convenient time than right now. Or will you move on and ignore the call of Christ? Will you accept Jesus as your Lord and Savior or will you find yourself abandoned by God? The choice is yours right now.

Scriptures to enjoy:

2 Corinthians 6:2
Romans 13:11-14

Prayer: Jesus, it is my prayer that no one will ignore Your call on their life. I pray that all will come to repentance and accept You as Lord and Savior. Amen.

What's Stopping You?

What's stopping you from saying "yes" to Jesus?
Is it your fear or your pride? Your busyness worldly preoccupation? Your sin?
What could be more important than your eternal soul?

Nothing is too difficult for God. "I am the Lord, the God of all mankind; is there anything too hard for me?" Jeremiah 32:27 (TLB)
He can heal your broken heart, cure your painful memories, encourage your righteous ambitions.

But first you must say "yes" to His soft spoken offer of salvation. Jesus died for your reconciliation with the Father. And nothing can ever separate you from God's love. But the choice to say "yes" is yours. So what's stopping you? Your eternity depends on it.

Scriptures to enjoy:

Luke 1:37
Romans 8:37-39
Jeremiah 32:27

Prayer: Lord, thank You for saving me and providing me an eternal home with You. May others find You too. In Jesus' precious name. Amen.

What Heaven Is

Heaven is our home as Christians. It is where Jesus reigns and we will one day reign there with Him. Eternity is extending on and on forever, never ending. To share it with Jesus is what I long for. The fact that I get to share it with others who love Jesus also makes my heavenly eternity a wonderful prospect.

Eternal life begins here on earth when we accept Christ as our personal Savior. The Holy Spirit begins to teach us what the Lord has for us as we read and mediate on the Word of God, fellowship with other believers, and pray in Jesus' Name.

So while we are on earth we have a job to do that the Holy Spirit will lead us to, a unique ministry prepared for us to complete as we daily walk with Him. When our task is done and Jesus comes for us or calls us home, we will begin our eternity with Him in that home He has prepared for us in heaven.

Scriptures to enjoy:

Isaiah 57:14-16
John 14:1-6

Prayer: Jesus, thank You for making eternity with You possible through Your death on the cross. Thank You for preparing a place for me and all believers in heaven that we may be with you forever. Amen.

What Have I Lost?

By surrendering to Jesus what have I lost? Certainly not my identity, because in Him I am complete. I have not lost my personal abilities since He gave me all the gifts I have so I can do what He has called me to do. I did not lose my freedom because Christ has set me free.

I haven't lost my sustenance for I have all I need. I have not lost my love of people. My circle of family and friends continues to grow as the brethren are joined together in common purpose here on earth—to share the Good News of Christ.

Let's see then what I did lose. I lost my sin. My guilt and shame are gone since that was associated with my sin. My longing for more possessions has left me because now I store up treasures in heaven. I have no more loneliness since Jesus is always with me by providing me His Holy Spirit Who is my constant Companion. My focus is clarified as in Him I dwell. His Holy Spirit gives me direction so my purpose is clear. So it seems I have lost nothing I wanted to keep and I have kept only what matters most: my life in Christ and it extends to my eternity with Him.

Scriptures to enjoy:

John 3:16
Galatians 1:3-5
Acts 2:38
Matthew 6:19-21
John 14:15-17

Prayer: Lord, I pray that others may lose themselves in You that they too may dwell with You forever. Thank you for Your gift of eternal life through Christ our Lord. Amen.

What Do You Call the Baby?

Many years ago my niece had a solo part in a Christmas play. "What's the Baby's name?" was the song her little girl voice sang out loud and clear. She knew His name was "Jesus" then and now she's all grown up with a little girl of her own. The names both of us claim for the Baby in the manger at Christmas reflect who He is in our lives every day: Wonderful Counselor, Prince of Peace, Almighty, Emmanuel, Mighty God, Jesus to name just a few. What do you call the one who reigns in your heart today? Do you know this Baby born in a manger called Jesus? Is Jesus the King in your home and in your life? If He is not you can ask Him to be right now. He wants to rule in your life too as He does in the hearts of all His children at Christmas and every day all the year through.

Scriptures to enjoy:

Isaiah 9:3-7
Matthew 1:22-23

Prayer: Thank You, Lord, for being the King of Glory who comes to us by our invitation and leads us in every action, every day. Be the Prince of Peace in my life always. In the precious name of Jesus. Amen.

What Are You Doing With Your Talent?

The Lord gives each of us an appointed amount to work with—skills, abilities, aptitudes, money, time. These are referred to as talents. We all receive these from Christ (the Master). He has provided for our care. Everyone has at least one "talent" illustrated in the scriptures. Some of us have more. We can use the talent to multiply blessing to those around us or we can bury it in the ground, hide it or otherwise thwart its growth. It is given to everyone according to his abilities. "And unto one he gave five talents, to another two, and to another one; to every man according to his several ability; and straightway took his journey.." Matthew 25:15 (KJV)

As we await Christ's return, we have an account to use in His absence. In this parable there were three people given something to work with. Two received praise from the Lord when He returned, but not the third. Two used their "talents" but the third did not. The question for each of us is what are you doing with your talent? You will have to give an accounting of how you've used it. Start today using whatever you have been given in the service of Christ's kingdom. He is coming back!

"I am the Alpha and the Omega—the beginning and the end," says the Lord God. "I am the one who is, who always was, and who is still to come—the Almighty One." Revelation 1:8 (NLT)

Scriptures to enjoy:

Matthew 25:14-30
Romans 12:6-8
Revelation 1:8

Prayer: Thank You, Jesus, for blessing me. Help me to use the gifts You've given me to benefit Your kingdom daily. In Your name, I pray. Amen.

We Are Not Defenseless

It seems like we no longer have a voice in our nation's policies. Sometimes we feel helpless to change things in our lives that we don't like. Some days it appears that everything is snowballing out of control around us or maybe even in us. It is especially at those times we need to remember the words of Scripture: "If God is for us. who can be against us?" Romans 8:31 (NKJV)

God has given us His defenses. He has provided us a way out of every temptation (1 Corinthians 10:13) and has promised to always be with us (Matthew 28:20). If God raised Jesus from the dead, and He did, He conquered death. Then what enemy or issue can be too great for Him to handle for us? Our problem is that we try to "deal" with things in our own strength rather than to rely on the Lord. Jesus said, "Come to Me, all you who labor and are heavy laden, and I will give you rest. Take My yoke upon you and learn from Me, for I am gentle and lowly in heart, and you will find rest for your souls. For My yoke is easy and My burden is light." Matthew 11:28-30 (NKJV)

Therefore, we have One who stands in the gap for us in all things. We are not defenseless. We have The Defender on our side and we win. Call upon His name and be saved.

Romans 8:29-39
Proverbs 18:10
1 Corinthians 10:13
Matthew 28:20
Matthew 11:28-30
1 Peter 5:6-8

Prayer: Jesus, thank You for being my Defender against the evils of this world. Help me always to come to You for whatever I need. Amen.

Wake Up, O Church of God!

Over the last few weeks I've been learning several things in my Bible study. One important truth that came like a revelation to me was how complacent we can become in our "church" activities. In reading the messages to the churches in John's Revelation I was struck by the compromising actions of these churches. All began well spreading the Good News of Christ. But they began to compromise the truth of God's word with the standards of their cultures. How like the churches in our country today. We wonder why we aren't growing, bringing in new members, and thriving because we are filled with activities. But are the activities those lead by the Truth, guided by the Holy Spirit? Too often today we accept atmosphere or ambiance in our "worship" and never invite God to the services. We are simply too busy trying to fit in, or not offend, or show that we can be tolerant, to adhere to what Jesus taught us.

One thing that is clear in these scriptures in Revelation is that Jesus is reaching out to the churches with the message: "Anyone with ears to hear must listen to the Spirit and understand what he is saying to the churches…" Revelation 2:7 (NLT) This message was directed to the church at Ephesus, but is repeated to each of the seven first century churches. While it is directed to the early church the message applies to the churches in America today. We are called to repent and obey what the Word of God teaches. If that means we must change the way we are doing things, let the Holy Spirit lead. If we don't, the warnings are clear: "…I will come to you quickly and remove your lampstand from its place—unless you repent." Revelation 2:5b (NKJV)

The Lord gives us clear guidelines: listen, hear, repent, return. If our churches and the members therein, don't return to the teaching of the Scriptures and follow them, we will not be effective in winning souls to the Lord and people will go to hell. The choice is ours. What will we do?

Jesus says: "Behold, I stand at the door and knock. If anyone hears My voice and opens the door, I will come in to him and dine with him, and he with Me." Revelation 3:20 (NKJV)

We are overcomers; we will walk with Him in white! Praise the Lord!

Scriptures to enjoy:

Revelation 2-3
John 14:6
Revelation 21:3-4
Revelation 12:11

Prayer: Thank You, Jesus, for Your sacrifice for me. Thank You, Holy Spirit, for guiding me. May I walk on the path where You lead. In Jesus's precious Name. Amen.

Waiting and Watching

Waiting and wondering what God must do
To make His impression firmly on you.

Waiting and watching as your life unfurls
Knowing God's plan is perfect and good.

Waiting and praying you will know Him too
And come to this Light as you really should.

Waiting and knowing God is greater than all your sin
With Him all things work for your good if in Him you believe.

Waiting and loving you just as I do
Expecting great things that only God can reveal.

Waiting and believing that as on Him you rely
All things painful are finely denied.

Waiting and knowing His timing is perfect and
In Christ all things are possible for those who trust Him.

Waiting and watching for you to abide
In Christ the only Person who can turn the tide.

Waiting and knowing that in Him you will find
Peace and joy if you put your hand in His.

Waiting and watching for you to accept Him
And cast your burdens aside to rest in His love.

Scriptures to enjoy:

Psalm 149:4
Matthew 19:23-26
Matthew 9:23
1 Peter 5:6-11
Romans 8:28-39

Prayer: Thank You, Jesus, for leading us to You. Help my family to all find salvation by Your grace. In Your name, I pray. Amen.

Vacation

Have you ever just wanted to relax and think about nothing in particular? To go on a vacation that separated you from all responsibilities and daily cares and concerns? I have searched the scriptures and I found only two references that used the word "vacation" and that was in The Message. One is where Herod is said to have taken a vacation when the jailor couldn't produce Peter from the jail (Acts 12:18-19) and the other is when Elijah, speaking to the prophets of Baal, suggests maybe he (their god) is on vacation when he doesn't respond to their pleas (1 Kings 18:27-28). Jesus never took a vacation. He was about His Father's business all of His earthly life. My conclusion is that since we are to be imitators of Christ we too should be about the Father's business daily.

Now this doesn't mean we shouldn't rest to refresh ourselves. Jesus did go away by Himself to rest and pray. The message to me is that if I need rest I should incorporate praying into my rest. This will not only refresh my body but regenerate my spirit.

So before planning a "vacation," think about what you expect to accomplish. And if you are trying to escape from something it probably won't happen; you'll have to come back one day. If you need to be refreshed by more time alone with the Savior then spend that time with Him. Take time to pray and relax with Jesus. You won't have to take a vacation. He is with you always.

Scriptures to enjoy:

Luke 2:40-49
Ephesians 5:1-2
1 Kings 18:27-28
Luke 5:16
Luke 6:12

Prayer: Dear Jesus, thank You for refreshing me when I need it. Help me to relax in You always. Amen.

Use Your Day Wisely

Our days are numbered. In other words, we will all die someday. Two questions arise: what will we do with the days we have and where we will spend our eternity? Are we using our time to share the Word of God, the Good News that Jesus came to be our Savior and restore a right relationship with God? Are we telling others the message that God loves us and wants us to live with Him forever in heaven when our numbered days are done? Or do we spend our days accumulating things and gaining wealth or power? Do we strive to outdo the neighbors or get one up on our competition. Only what we do for the Lord will last. So use your time well. Make it count for Jesus because He has made it all possible for you. Your life as you know it here and now and the eternity you will have with Him after you pass from this life.

You must decide where you will spend your eternity. If you never choose Jesus as your Lord and Savior you will be eternally separated from Him and spend that eternity in hell. If you accept His free gift of salvation and opt to follow Him on the path He designed for you your eternity will be forever with Him in heaven.

So chose now. "But if you are unwilling to obey the Lord, then decide today whom you will obey. ...But as for me and my family, we will serve the Lord." Joshua 24:15a, c (TLB)

Don't waste a minute of your life, because your days are numbered. "Right now God is ready to welcome you. Today he is ready to save you." 2 Corinthians 6:2b (TLB)

Scriptures to enjoy:

2 Peter 3:7-9
Joshua 24:14-21
2 Corinthians 6:1-2

Prayer: Thank You, Jesus, for giving me this day and each day of my life. May I use it to serve You only every day. In Your Name. Amen.

To Be Like Peter—Or Not

Peter often spoke out; without thinking or inappropriately. At Jesus' trial before His crucifixion Peter denied even knowing Jesus, but at least he said something. Other disciples had run away entirely. Peter's denial of Christ allowed him to be corrected by the Lord after the Lord's resurrection. Peter was teachable. He was willing to follow Jesus and learn what the Lord wanted him to do. Peter was used by God to teach others, to heal and to save many. Peter was open and willing to speak. What about me? Am I willing to share Jesus? If not, why not?

Scriptures to enjoy:

Matthew 17:1-6
Mark 14:66-72
Matthew 16:22-23
Mark 8:31-33
John 21:15-19
Acts 4:1-4
Mark 8:38

Prayer: Thank You, Jesus, for the example of Peter. May I always be willing to speak as the Holy Spirit leads me so that others may know of You. In Your name, I pray. Amen.

The Little Things

What do you consider to be the little things in your life? Are they the small things that make you smile like the licks from a wet puppy tongue, a friend's smile, a good score on an assignment at school, your child saying "I love you" or any other of a hundred other things we think are incidental in our days of busyness. But it's these "little things" that make our lives meaningful and that God continues to bless us with. Are we counting our blessings as God counts them? Do we admire the flowers in bloom or the soft breeze on our faces? Do we grumble and complain at the slow moving traffic or count the blessings that we have a car, can drive it, or have roads on which to move? Annoyances abound. But blessings are bountiful and make our lives so rich.

Count the little blessings today for God has provided each one; they are His gifts to you. "Blessed is the people of whom this is true; blessed is the people whose God is the LORD!" Psalm 144:15 (NIV)

Scriptures to enjoy:

Psalm 144
Habakkuk 3:17-19
James 1:17

Prayer: Thank You, Jesus, for all the blessings you give me every day. Help me to be grateful. In Your Name I pray. Amen.

The Joy of Jesus

Do I have the joy of Jesus in my life? If I do there are ways that others can see it. The Holy Spirit is the Guide for believers and will lead us in showing this joy as we walk our daily paths. But we must first invite Him to be the Leader, then we must be willing to follow on the path He shows us. If we do our lives will reflect to others Jesus living in us.

As Christ followers we have the joy of Jesus. The real question is does it show? If it does scripture tells us that we will walk wisely, redeem the time, understand what the will of the Lord is, sing and make melody to the Lord, give thanks, and be respectful and courteous to others. (Ephesians 5:14-20) Do others see me doing those things? Am I doing them? Or am I the grumbler and complainer that walks in the ways of the world, showing dissatisfaction over others I encounter or activities I don't like? Forbid it, Lord.

"The revelation of GOD is whole and pulls our lives together. The signposts of GOD are clear and point out the right road. The life-maps of GOD are right, showing the way to joy. The directions of GOD are plain and easy on the eyes. GOD's reputation is twenty-four-carat gold, with a lifetime guarantee. The decisions of GOD are accurate down to the nth degree." Psalm 19:7-9 (MSG)

Scriptures to enjoy:

Psalm 19:7-9
Habakkuk 3:17-19

Ephesians 5:14-20
Galatians 5:19-23
1 John 1:1-4

Prayer: Forgive me Lord, when I don't reflect the joy that I have in my heart from knowing You. May I "walk circumspectly" with You daily as the Holy Spirit leads me forward. In Jesus' precious name. Amen.

The Earth Is Not Flat

In 1492 Christopher Columbus sailed for what he believed would be a new world during a time when most of the people of the society thought the world had an edge. They believed he would sail off the ends of the earth never to be heard from again. Columbus later returned from his voyage proving that there was no edge, at least not as far as he had sailed. Later in 1519 an explorer, Ferdinand Magellan, organized a fleet of ships that would become the first Europeans to circumnavigate the earth proving conclusively that the earth was not flat as believed.

Today there are people who do not believe hell is a real place. There will be no proof positive of this for humans since no one will ever visit there and return to tell of it. There is scripture to tell us a little about hell in Luke's gospel. Luke says: "And in hell he lift up his eyes, being in torments, and seeth Abraham afar off, and Lazarus in his bosom. And he cried and said, Father Abraham, have mercy on me, send Lazarus, that he may dip the tip of his finger in water, and cool my tongue; for I am tormented in this flame." Luke 16:23b-24 (KJV)

There are others who do not believe heaven is a real place either. But again scripture tells us about heaven: "… behold, a throne was set in heaven, and one sat on the throne. And he that sat was to look upon like a jasper and a sardine stone: and there was a rainbow round about the throne, in sight like unto an emerald. And round about the throne were four and twenty seats: and upon the seats I saw four and twenty elders sitting, clothed in white raiment; and they had on their heads crowns of gold. And out of the throne proceeded lightnings and thunderings and voices…" Revelation 4:2b-5a (KJV)

Both the description of heaven and of hell assumes a belief in the scriptures as the Word of God. Do you believe in the Word of God? Do you believe in hell? Do you believe in heaven? If you were to consider where you spend eternity which image would you prefer to inhabit? The reality of God's word is that "Everyone who calls on the Lord will be saved." Romans 10:13 (NLT) The choice is yours, but remember the earth is not flat.

Scriptures to enjoy:

Luke 16:19-31
Revelation 4:2-5
Romans 10:8-13
Luke 13:24-30
Revelation 21:1-4

Prayer: Lord, I pray no one will reject the truth of Your Word. May all repent and come to salvation through Christ, in Whose name I pray. Amen.

The Creator

A recent visit to the majestic Tetons and the splendor of the Yellowstone geysers reminded me again of how great God is. There is so much beauty in the nature God created for us to enjoy the list could go on for pages. Consider the sky at night filled with uncounted numbers of stars or the sunrise in the morning. What are the things you consider beautiful that you see around you, people, animals, flowers? God made it all. We should praise Him for that alone. But He did more.

God sent His Son Jesus to be the sacrifice for us that would bring us reconciliation with the Father. With this our futures are secure in heaven if we accept Jesus as our Lord and Savior, confess our sin and turn from it to follow the new path that the Holy Spirit will provide for everyone who makes the decision to follow Jesus as Lord. The Creator of all the beauty we see around us is the One who created a place in heaven for us. God made the creation but the adoration comes from us. Some never see the beauty around them. The acceptance of eternity with Christ is our choice but some will never make that choice. What about you? Have you decided to follow Jesus? Why not do it today?

Scriptures to enjoy:

Genesis 1:1-27, 31
Colossians 1:15-17
John 3: 16-17
1 Peter 2:9-10

Prayer: Lord Jesus, give us eyes to see the beauty You have provided for us on this earth. Give us hearts that long to follow you as Savior and Lord. In that Name that is above all names, Jesus. Amen.

The Battle is the Lord's

Satan is subtle. He doesn't launch a frontal attack when a backdoor approach will work. Instead he attacks each of us where we are most vulnerable. He puts little thoughts into our heads that cause us to question what scripture says or he offers us compromises in what we know is wrong action. He doesn't bring out the big guns when small problems will undo us. For example people who are allergic to peanuts aren't even tempted to bring them into their houses. But they may not be allergic to chocolate so they buy it only to be tempted to eat it when they shouldn't. Likewise Satan won't tempt you with things that don't appeal to you (like the peanuts) but he will taunt you with things that entice you (like the chocolate). But rejoice because the battle we are fighting isn't against flesh and blood but against the forces of darkness and the Lord fights for you and me and He wins.

So remember when you are threatened with a small skirmish in your life or what seems like an insurmountable war, the battle is the Lord's and He wins. Satan is defeated forever. Don't limit God's victories for you. Take Him at His word. The battle is His and He wins.

Scriptures to enjoy:

2 Chronicles 20:15
Ephesians 6:12
Revelation 20:10

Prayer: Lord, thank You for always being on my side and fighting the battles for me. Help me to rely always on You. Amen.

Take Off Your Shoes

I live in a desert region and while the ground isn't necessarily productive with farm crops some things grow here. Things like thistle, puncture weeds and other noxious things. If you mistakenly walk on the ground without shoes on you'll be picking puncture weed stickers out of your feet for weeks to say nothing of the pain you'll experience.

Moses herded his father-in-law's sheep in a desert region not too much different than the one I live in. There must have been enough scrub grass for the sheep to survive on but I can imagine sage brush and weeds too. Moses saw a unique sight when he saw a burning bush. Now I can imagine spontaneous combustion burning something. I've seen it happen to hay and straw stacks in extreme heat or when they are too moist when stacked. So a burning bush I can imagine in the desert heat and dryness. But the bush Moses saw burning was not consumed and the fire didn't spread. In dry areas like mine if something starts to burn it immediately spreads to everything around it and blacked cinders are all that remain when it is out. The bush Moses observed neither blackened, nor spread the fire, nor was turned to ash.

Being curious, Moses went to see why this phenomenon occurred. It was at that moment that God spoke to him and told Moses to take off his shoes. That meant standing barefoot in the weeds, stickers and dirt. Moses didn't question God only obeyed.

When God commands me to do something that doesn't make sense to me or fit in with my plans or it seems unpleasant (like standing barefooted in the weeds) do I do as Moses did and comply with God's request? Or do I rationalize and make excuses or ignore the things I am commanded to do?

God protected Moses's feet from the weeds and stickers. God led him to complete the task He had for him, namely to guide the Israelites out of Egypt. Likewise, He will protect and provide for me. But I must take the first step of faith and remove my shoes. Am I willing to trust God? Or am I more confident in my own abilities? I'm ready to take off my shoes. Are you? Paul states: "For I can do everything through Christ, who gives me strength." Philippians 4:13 (NLT)

Scriptures to enjoy:

Exodus 3:1-10
Philippians 4:4-13

Prayer: Jesus, it is only through You can I do anything. Use me today as I am willing to take off my shoes if that is what You command. Amen.

Take Each Day

I had reached the end of my fragile balance between handling daily pressures and feeling totally out of control. I was out of control on all fronts. Tears streamed down my face and I felt like God had deserted me. After all He'd promised if we asked in faith, He would grant our petitions. "In that day you will no longer ask me anything. Very truly I tell you, my Father will give you whatever you ask in my name." John 16:23 (NIV) I had not only asked, but I had begged for things to get better in my life. Yet here I was.

It was then, in my desperation, that I could see clearly my dependence only on the Father. Nothing else could make things better. I certainly couldn't do anything more. The whole burden had to be given to the Lord. Once I gave it unconditionally to Him, He could handle it on my behalf. But as long as I kept something under my thumb God's glory couldn't be seen and He couldn't work in my life.

Today wasn't perfect. It wasn't even good but it was better and I can see the Lord anew at work in my life as I live according to His will and not my own.

Scriptures to enjoy:

John 16:23
2 Corinthians 4:16
1 Peter 5:6-7

Prayer: Thank You, Father, for helping me always. Amen.

Subtle Beauty

Subtle beauty shines as soft colors fill the sky at sunrise,
Not flamboyant colors, just muted tones spreading as morning breaks.
How like a life lived in Christ.

As Christ spreads His love through every part of us,
We can share with others the strength that He provides.
We don't have to be flashy speakers or excellent singers, or famed artists,
Only constant, kindly, compassionate bearers of Christ spreading in the world.

Scriptures to enjoy:

Psalm 8
Psalm 96:6

Prayer: Jesus, Creator of all things, thank You for the beauty and blessings You surround us with. May we appreciate what You provide and be good stewards for what You give us. Amen.

Solution to Troubles Today

What troubles you today? Fear of failure or losing your job or spouse? Disobedient children? Hurt feelings from cruel words? Financial distress? Out of control, destructive habits of drug or alcohol abuse? No matter what your problem is a relationship with God is the solution. God doesn't take troubles away in our lives but He gives us a way to handle them. So call on Jesus and let the Holy Spirit lead you in the way you should go in each situation. Peace that passes all understanding can be yours if you trust in the Lord Jesus Christ right now. Call on the Name of Jesus and be saved.

Scriptures to enjoy:

James 1:2-4
John 15:4-5
1 Peter 1:2

Prayer: Thank You, Jesus, that Your peace may be ours if we ask for it, that You will guide us through all circumstances in our lives and provide for our needs. Help us to trust in You in all things. In Your name, Jesus. Amen.

Sin

What does sin look like in your life? Do you recognize sin in your life? Or do you rationalize it or try to justify it with endless explanations? Or do you compare yourself to other people and think you're not so bad when compared to them? After all you don't do anything that bad.

If you recognize sin in your life what have you done about it? Do you try to hide it? Do you think you can hide it from God even if you can hide it from people? Or do you work harder or do more to try to make amends for what you have done wrong?

Do you admit you are a sinner? Do you compare yourself to Christ rather than other people? Do you confess your sins when you fall short and allow the grace of Jesus to cover you and move you forward as you seek to draw nearer to the Risen Lord Who offers us pardon whenever we admit the mistakes? Only He can restore us to a right relationship with the Father and only when we bring our sin to Him for forgiveness.

In the world today temptations to sin are all around us and it is easy to ignore the Truth as presented in the Bible. We are all sinners in need of the Savior. "For everyone has sinned; we all fall short of God's glorious standard." Romans 3:23 (NLT)

Jesus invites us all but He waits for us to accept. Admit your sin, confess it to Him now and accept the peace only He can bring to you. " But if we confess our sins to him, he is faithful and just to forgive us our sins and to cleanse us from all wickedness." 1 John 1:9 (NLT) Begin your new life today. "This means that anyone who belongs to Christ has become a new person. The old life is gone; a new life has begun!" 2 Corinthians 5:17 (NLT)

Scriptures to enjoy:

Luke 18:13-14
1 John 1:9
Psalm 51:1-10
2 Corinthians 5:17

Prayer: Thank You, Jesus, for Your forgiveness of my sin. Guide me in my new life in You. Amen.

Shelter in the Storm

Outside the clouds looked angry and menacing as they scuttled across the grey-black sky. The winds howled as they buffeted whatever got in their path. The pounding of the rain on the windows made going beyond the doorway forbidding. Even the animals were driven inside to shelter. As I looked out the window I was glad to be in the warm safety of the house rather that out in the midst of the storm.

The storm reminded me of my walk on this earth. Frequently there are storms on the way. There are relationships that are challenged by the culture in which we live. There are finances that are destroyed by irresponsibility on our parts or through no fault of our own in the loss of a job or provider. Loved ones die and we are left sad and alone. But in all the hardships we face in the lives we lead, God is faithful to provide shelter for us. In His Word we are reminded: "From the end of the earth I will cry to You, when my heart is overwhelmed; Lead me to the rock that is higher than I. For You have been a shelter for me, a strong tower from the enemy. I will abide in Your tabernacle forever; I will trust in the shelter of Your wings. Selah." Psalm 61:2-4 (NKJV)

So no matter what terrors or storms of life surround you, you can say with the psalmist: "Cause me to hear Your loving kindness in the morning, for in You do I trust; Cause me to know the way in which I should walk, for I lift up my soul to You. Deliver me, O LORD, FROM MY ENEMIES; In You I take shelter." Psalm 143:8-9 (NKJV) All we have to do is call out to the Lord and He will protect us.

I am confident in the deliverance of the Lord from whatever befalls me because like David I claim His promise: "The LORD is my rock and my fortress and my deliverer; My God, my strength, in whom I will trust; My shield and the horn of my salvation, my stronghold." Psalm 18:2 (NKJV) And with the apostle Paul I say: "And He said to me, "My grace is sufficient for you, for My strength is made perfect in weakness." Therefore most gladly I will rather boast in my infirmities, that the power of Christ may rest upon me." 2 Corinthians 12:9 (NKJV)

Praise God, He is my Rock!

Scriptures to enjoy:

Psalm 91:1-2
Psalm 61:1-8
Psalm 143:8-9
2 Corinthians 12:9

Prayer: Jesus, thank You that You are the stronghold of my life and that You will not be shaken, no matter what comes along. Amen.

Share God's Love

Tonight I watched a beautiful full moon get swallowed up ever so gradually by clouds that eventually completely blocked the light and beauty of the moon. This scene reminded me of how sin in my life can insidiously infiltrate until it dilutes my witness and consumes my effectiveness.

But like the breath of wind that drove away the shroud of clouds that covered the full moon, the freshening of the Holy Spirit can dispel the darkness of sin in which we become enveloped. When we call on Jesus and confess our sin, "He is faithful and just to forgive us our sins and to cleanse us from all unrighteousness." 1 John 1:9 (KJV) Then our lights can shine brightly in a world clamoring for the love we share from our Savior as we walk in His light.

Scriptures to enjoy:

Isaiah 50:9-10
1 John 1:7

Prayer: Lord and Savior, thank You for filling me with Your Holy Spirit as I seek you. May I be a light for Jesus daily in this world of darkness. May the love You share with me be shared with everyone I meet. In Jesus' name. Amen.

Sandpaper

I have used sandpaper many times to smooth wood or prepare a wall for paint or to remove rust from tools. In each case it is to help bring out the usefulness or beauty of the object being sanded. Recently in a Bible study I participate in someone mentioned that we are like sandpaper to others sometimes. As I contemplated that in my life I realized there are many ways to gain the desired end as we assist others in their spiritual growth and walk with the Lord.

I'm sure there have been people I rubbed the wrong way when they misunderstood something I said, or maybe I was just plain rude to someone. But that wasn't the meaning in this discussion. In this situation we were talking about helping each other to smooth rough edges. That brings out the best in another person as we talk over the meanings of scripture or how best to witness to someone else or to be used by God. The key is in the willingness of each one to be shaped and changed.

We have a responsibility to help others as we are called to meet their needs. We can be an accountability factor for prayer partners or a sounding board for ideas in scripture. We are God's workmen to be used as He sees fit. But we must be available if called to be the sandpaper for others.

Scriptures to enjoy:

Proverbs 27:17
Psalms 7:9-11
Hebrews 10:23-25

Prayer: Lord, help me to be sensitive to the needs of others that I may be "sandpaper" if needed and "iron" when appropriate. Give me discernment to know the difference in the needs. Amen.

Riding the Waves

The troughs climb higher and higher
The depths are so low
The water grows higher the deeper I fall.
It closes around me as the darkness engulfs.
My heart is racing as down I go.
It seems nothing can stop the roar of the waves.
My lips move silently as to the grave I am drawn.
If ever I needed you, my God, it's now.
Save me from drowning in this sea of pain.
My heart's cry is never again will I be so foolish
As to abandon the shore of Your outstretched hand
To wander into the crashing surf
With troubles and trials while I walk this earth.
But as on You I lean, my legs are steady
And the waves can't hurt me.
So let me always ride the waves with You as my Guide.
No longer alone
No fear shall I face
When I turn to You and your matchless grace.
The tides will ebb and the tides will flow
But my soul is assured a mansion in heaven as on You I rely.
Sheltered from the rising water
Protected from harm by your steadfast love
Safe from riding the waves of sin and distress
When I am called to my mansion of rest
And spend eternity surrounded by Your Light and Your Love.

Scriptures to enjoy:

2 Samuel 22:4-6
Isaiah 43:1-3
Jeremiah 29:11-13
Mark 4:36-40

Prayer: Dear Lord, thank You for calming the storms in my life and protecting me from the disasters that are often of my own making. Help me to follow You more closely as I walk the path before me. In Jesus' name. Amen.

Resurrection Day

Consider this truth: Death is really just the beginning of our lives. Our eternal life with Christ begins at the moment of death. So why does death make us sad? It makes us sad because for those of us still living we are in grief over the loss we are experiencing. But for that person who is now in the very presence of the Savior, the life they now have is what all believers are waiting for. We long to be in the presence of Jesus.

Think of this: Jesus Himself was challenged by the religious leaders of His day. He was threatened, tempted, tried and convicted of crimes He never committed. But He was willing to go to the cross and die for you and me to bring us back into a right relationship with God the Father. He didn't try to get out of this world without pain and suffering. He simply lived as the Father commanded. His resurrection conquered death. Scripture says that Christ was the first to be raised then all who believe will be raised 1 Corinthians 15:20 (NLT) " But in fact, Christ has been raised from the dead. He is the first of a great harvest of all who have died."

In speaking to Martha, Jesus said: "I am the resurrection and the life. He who believes in Me, though he may die, he shall live. And whoever lives and believes in Me shall never die." John 11:25-26 (NKJV)

So while we mourn for the loss of the presence of our loved ones at death, we shall rejoice at that glad reunion in heaven when we will see them and Christ face to face. That will be our resurrection day and the start of an eternity with our Savior. "For he has rescued us from the kingdom of darkness and transferred us into the Kingdom of his dear Son, who purchased our freedom and forgave our sins." 1 Corinthians 15:13 (NLT)

Praise God. Start rejoicing now.

Scriptures to enjoy:

Philippians 2:5-11
1 Corinthians 15:13-20
John 11:25-26
Colossians 1:13-17

Prayer: Lord, my desire is to be with You in heaven. But for now You have a purpose for me to be here on earth. Help me to be faithful to Your calling that others may see You in me. In Jesus's name I pray. Amen.

Remember, Redeemed, Resurrected

Remember Whose you are
    God remembered me when He created the world
    Christ remembered me as He died on Calvary's tree
    I must remember the things Jesus has patiently taught to me

Redeemed are the saints

    God planned for me to be redeemed when He sent Jesus to the world
    Jesus meant for all to be redeemed when He died a sinner's death
    I am redeemed through His plan of salvation when I surrender my will

Resurrected to reign eternally

    God resurrected His Son to conquer death and hell
    Jesus was resurrected to give me eternal life
    I will be resurrected to share heaven with Jesus when He calls me home.

Therefore, I remember that I am redeemed to be resurrected by the victory of the King.

Scriptures to enjoy:

Deuteronomy 6:7
1 Corinthians 11:23-25
Galatians 3:11-14
Philippians 3:10-11

Prayer: Jesus, You are my King. Thank You for redeeming me and promising me victory over death in the resurrection. Help me always to remember to put You on the throne of my life. Amen.

Rely on the Lord in the Relay of Life

Rely on the Lord or deny your responsibilities
As you assume your role in this life.
Expect challenges, some easy some hard,
As you endure and extend the limits you can achieve.
Let others give aid
As you live TODAY, not yesterday or tomorrow.
Yearn to serve God the best that you can
As you make the most of your relay in this life.

Scriptures to enjoy:

Ecclesiastes 3:11
Hebrews 13:8
John 16:33

Prayer for today: Dear Lord, thank You for providing a plan for my life. Help me to allow Your Holy Spirit to work in my life that I may serve You the way You intended for me to do. Amen.

Redeeming the Time

Do you ever wish you had more time in a day because you have so much to get done? I know I do. We all have the same amount of time. That same amount of time is what the Lord had in His day. So what are we doing with the time the Lord has given to us?

One important thing our Lord did was pray. So that should be one of our priorities. We can pray in any place at any time for anything. We can redeem some of our time waiting at a red light or in the grocery line by praying rather than getting impatient or letting our mind wander.

The Lord also always had time for those who needed His help. So it seems people should be as important to us and we should render aid and assistance whenever it may be needed with an attitude of love and service, redeeming the time from resentment and feeling put out.

The Lord sought time alone to rest and refresh. We should allow ourselves time alone especially alone with the Lord. We should not be so "busy" we neglect our health because we don't rest properly. We should provide refreshment physically as well as spiritually in order to be prepared each day for what the Lord leads us to.

As we allow the Holy Spirit to be our Guide, physically and spiritually for the daily challenges we can redeem the time from what we might waste it on. The Spirit will lead us if we only ask.

Expect to be lead as you submit to His will and allow Him to show you the best use of your time today. You will be blessed.

Scriptures to enjoy:

James 4:7
1 Peter 5:6-7
Matthew 5:1-16
Ephesians 2:8-10

Prayer: Lord, help me to use my time wisely as You lead me daily on the path You have chosen for me. In Jesus' name. Amen.

Red Letter Words

Out of words written in **red**
Jesus calls for me.
He says, **"I am the Way, the Truth and the Life."**
He did it all for me.

Out of words written in **red**
Jesus calls for you.
The Savior says, **"I am the Resurrection and the Life."**
He did it all for you.

Out of words written in **red**
Jesus calls for us.
The Comforter says, **"Come unto me all you who labor
And are heavy laden,
And I will give you rest."**
He did it all for us.

Out of words written in **red**
Jesus calls the world.
The Master says, **"I have overcome the world."**
He did it all for the world.

Out of words written in **red**
Jesus promises to return.
The Redeemer says, **"I will come again and receive you unto myself."**
Because His promises are true
He will return.

Out of words written in **red**
Our Friend asks, "***Who do you say I am?***"
What is your answer?
What will you do with the words written in **red?**

Out of words written in **red**
The Savior is waiting for you.
He did it all for you.

Scriptures to enjoy:

John 14:6
Luke 11:25
Matthew 11:28
John 16:33
Revelation 22:7
Matthew 16:15

Prayer: Jesus, thank You for the gift of Your Words written for me out of Your love. Thank you for Your sacrifice that I may have eternal life. Amen.

Receive Your Sight

One story in the Bible tells about Jesus giving sight to a man who had been born blind. Jesus gave instructions to the man who would then receive his sight. The man who was healed was questioned by the religious leaders about the incident. The religious leaders wanted to disprove the miracle Jesus had performed. They asked the man where Jesus was and if he had really been blind before Jesus healed him. After repeatedly giving testimony he grew tired of the lack of understanding on the part of the religious leaders and responded with "…one thing I know, that, whereas I was blind, now I see." John 6:25b (KJV) The man had not only received physical sight but spiritual sight as well.

In these verses we see an illustration of ourselves. The blind man was told to go and wash and receive his sight. Jesus tells us over and over again to receive Him ourselves and we will be cleansed from our sin and unrighteousness. Far too often our response is like those around the blind man. When we are asked "Where is Jesus?" We reply, "I do not know" when our response should be "He lives in me and I have been washed clean by His blood."

If you haven't known the Savior won't you accept Him now and receive your sight? Do not be blind any longer. "Seek the Lord while He may be found, call upon Him while He is near." Isaiah 55:6 (KJV)

Scriptures to enjoy:

John 9:6-12
Isaiah 55:6-9

Prayer: Thank You, Lord, that You gave so freely that I can be pure, bathed by the blood, and can be declared blameless in Your sight because of Jesus' sacrifice. Amen.

Our Light

For several weeks the light in my microwave oven had not come on as it should have. I got used to the inconvenience and assumed it was a burned out bulb. It wasn't worth the effort to try to fix it. Then I spent a week involved in events that turned out less than what I had hoped they would be and definitely not what I had prayed they would be lie. As I reflected on this and just as I reached what felt like the bottom I prayed again, "God, what do you want me to do?"

As I was praying I was also using the malfunctioning microwave oven. As I pulled out the heated plate "something" made the light come back on. It wasn't really burned out. It dawned on me as that light came on that all the Father wants me to do is trust Him in His Word to Light my path. "Your Word is a lamp for my feet and a light to my path" according to the psalmist. Psalm 119:105 (NIV)

I am to remember that no matter how dark the circumstances "He will not leave me nor forsake me." Joshua 1:5 (NKJV) Jesus is the "Light of the world." John 8:12 (KJV)

Scriptures to enjoy:

John 8:12
Psalm 27:9
Psalm 119:105
John 1:1-9

Prayer: Lord, remind me that You are the Light of the World and want to light my way wherever I go. In Jesus' Name. Amen.

Opportunities

Opportunities to reach out,
to make a difference,
to change a life.

Opportunities to share the love,
to have the fellowship,
to meet the Savior.

Opportunities to break the bread,
to drink the cup,
to find forgiveness.

Opportunities to receive grace,
to be forgiven,
to know the Lord.

Opportunities to read the Word,
to grow in grace,
to live again forever with Christ.

Don't miss the opportunities.

Scriptures to enjoy:

Colossians 4:4-6
1 Corinthians 11:24-26

1 Corinthians 10:15-17
Mark 13:10-11

Prayer: Jesus, make me bold as You give me opportunities to share Your Gospel message with others. I pray in Your name. Amen.

New Beginnings

I've never liked fall. It seems so cold, dull and dark to me by comparison to the colors of spring and the warmth of summer. Due to the Lord's work in circumstances in my life I see this fall differently. Oh, the cool temperatures are definitely still there but I see the season in a new way.

Maybe it's the time in my life that the Lord is, but this season I'm seeing the autumn as a time of new beginnings and new opportunities. Rather than a season of disappointment and death, I'm seeing it as a time of newness in my life.

The Lord's mercies are new every day so I'm sure He can use the time of year to provide new opportunities for service and new dimensions of growth in my relationship with Him as I allow these new beginnings to take root.

Join me as I start today to walk more closely with the Savior and experience new beginnings with the new season of this year of life in Christ.

"This means that anyone who belongs to Christ has become a new person. The old life is gone; a new life has begun!" 2 Corinthians 5:17 (NLT)

Scriptures to enjoy:

Lamentations 3:20-26
2 Corinthians 5:16-20

Prayer: Lord, thank You for Your mercies toward me, for Your steadfast love and care. Guide me as I begin anew today. In Christ's name. Amen.

Mom, I love you today and always

You've always been there for me,
You've always been my friend.
I haven't always been so sweet, so kind, and loving when
As a stubborn child I spoke words disrespectfully said.

But in the good days and the bad,
You were there to hold my hand
And send me out again
Stronger, straighter, surer
No matter where I'd been.

You taught me how to be a friend
When to yield and when to bend
How to shelter others from the winds
Of unkind words and deeds
That would never bring joy only end in grief.

Your leadership and wisdom provided strength and growth
Your fellowship and hospitality for everyone was genuine
Your gentleness and love no one could ever challenge
Even in the difficulties of the sometimes chaos we knew as home.

There was a place for anyone who happened to show up.
You never knew how many places at the table on any given day.
For due to your example we might bring home a stray.
But no one was ever unwelcome and none were turned away.

Your energy was boundless in laundry,
Ironing and cooking.
You always had sewing project
Making gifts when we weren't looking.

A mother could never have been less appreciated
Than when she said "no you can't."
But sometimes that was sidestepped
If we bartered for more chores.

Teaching us the "how to dos" that every child must know
Must have been exhausting even for one like you.
None of us were eager to do the cleaning you required,
But somehow you managed to raise us and on our ways we go.

You set an example of compassion, commitment and humility
That I will always remember
For you alone are mother and you will always be
The first one I shall turn to whenever I need my friend.

If I've never said I'm sorry for all the grief I caused,
I say it now with heartfelt sorrow for all your time I wasted
In backtalk, arguments and rebellion.
I learned my lessons well.

But now I tell you truly from the bottom of my heart
No one could ever be a better friend to me
Nor a better mom than you.
Thank you for your patience, your loving and your support.
Thank you for being my friend, my example, and my mom.

Mom, I love you today and always with all that is in me
No one could have done more to bring me to where I've come.
Today as we celebrate you, Mom, know that you are loved.
Happy mother's day to my special mom,
And to moms everywhere.

Scriptures to enjoy:

Proverbs 31:10-31
Exodus 20:12

Prayer: Thank You, Lord, for my mother and for all the women in my life that have nurtured me. Thank You for the blessings of motherhood and for the love You provide for us. In Jesus' Name, I pray. Amen.

Ministry

Are you called to minister? I didn't ask if you were called to be a minister but to minister. You may say that's the job of the church or the pastor or someone else. But scripture makes it clear that it is the job of every believer to minister, which means to give aid, service or care to another. As a parent you do it for your children without thinking. You probably do it for your neighbors as the occasion arises. You think nothing of helping a friend out.

So why are we reluctant to answer the call of ministering to those in the world around us? Jesus commanded us to "love one another" (John 13:34) and sometimes we do. But for some reason the word "minister" feels threatening to us. It seems like it will make us vulnerable to ridicule or criticism from those we try to render aid to. The question is who are we trying to impress? The world or our Lord? Christ has called us to be His messengers. Listen to His word in Romans 1:16-17 (MSG) "It's news I'm most proud to proclaim, this extraordinary Message of God's powerful plan to rescue everyone who trusts him, starting with Jews and then right on to everyone else! God's way of putting people right shows up in the acts of faith, confirming what Scripture has said all along: "The person in right standing before God by trusting him really lives."''

But if we don't share this Message, the Good News of Christ's salvation for each of us, others may never hear it. It is our "ministry" as His representatives on earth to assist others in every way, including telling them what we know about the Savior. Don't assume someone else will be the one to "minister" to others. It is our privilege as Christ's representatives, His ministers, to fulfill the Great Commission: "Therefore, go and make disciples of all the nations, baptizing them in the name of the Father and the Son and the Holy Spirit. Teach these new disciples to obey all the commands I have given you. And be sure of this: I am with you always, even to the end of the age." Matthew 28:19-20 (NLT) Start right now.

Scriptures to enjoy:

Romans 1:16-17
Romans 10:14-16
Matthew 28:18-20
Psalm 103:20-22

Prayer: Thank You, Lord, for allowing me to serve You as Your representative among those I come in contact with. Make me more aware of the needs of others that I may minister in Your Name. In Christ, Whose Name I pray. Amen.

Memories

Why is it that most of us remember tragic events in our lives but we sometimes overlook the equally memorable blessings? Have we become so accustomed to the blessings that they become commonplace and we can assume they will continue? Many adults will recall vividly where they were and what they were doing when the Twin Towers were struck in New York City on Nine Eleven. We can recount the day when a loved one passed away. God can use these tragedies as blessings in our lives as well if we will allow Him to do so.

If you have children you can probably remember details of the days they were born. There are events in their lives that we relive in stories and videos too. But do we remember to thank God for each child each day? Do we recount the milestones with thanks or are we swallowed up in what they didn't do or what they did wrong?

The Lord gives us our memories to cherish that we may remember all He has done and provided for us. It is our responsibility to learn from all the events in our lives and it is important to our growing faith to praise God in all things, not just in the things we like. We are not to live in the past but to learn from what has transpired. But in all things to rejoice and give thanks for great are the blessings heaped upon each of us every day whether a day is memorable or mundane. There is a purpose for our lives each day and it is to glorify our Lord in all we say and do. Rejoice now!

Scriptures to enjoy:

1 Thessalonians 5:16-18
Philippians 4:4-8

Prayer: Dear Jesus, thank You for memories, good and bad. Help us to learn the lessons You want us to from each experience. May Your Holy Spirit lead us daily in the path You've chose for us that You may be gloried in our lives. In that Name above all names, Jesus Christ. Amen.

Make Every Drop Count

The western part of the United States has been suffering from a drought that has gone on for several years. (This is the year 2015.) Because of the water shortage there have been actions taken even at the state levels to make the most of the existing water. There is no way of knowing if these actions will be sufficient to maintain the water supply until the drought subsides. There is no way to predict even if there will be an end to the drought or if there will be real suffering such as food shortages and loss of life as a result. But people are learning to make every drop of their water count and not to waste even a little bit on unnecessary things.

Today we can remember what the scriptures tell us about the "living water" that Christ offers to everyone. We don't have to rely on governmental intervention or on our own conservation for the sustaining Life that comes from knowing Christ as Savior and Lord. Jesus, speaking to the Samaritan woman at the well said, ..."that people soon became thirsty again after drinking this water" "But the water I give them," he said, "becomes a perpetual spring within them, watering them forever with eternal life." John 4:13-14 (TLB)

So I encourage you to make every word and action count for the Lord. Waste no time today in whining or complaining, in regret or remorse for the "what might have beens" or the "if onlys" but "let us go right in to God himself, with true hearts fully trusting him to receive us because we have been sprinkled with Christ's blood to make us clean and because our bodies have been washed with pure water. Now we can look forward to the salvation God has promised us. There is no longer any room for doubt, and we can tell others that salvation is ours, for there is no question that he will do what he says." Hebrews 10:22-23 (TLB) Because in reality only what is done for Christ will matter and in the end. He will be our shepherd and "For the Lamb on the throne will be their Shepherd. He will lead them to springs of life-giving water. And God will wipe every tear from their eyes." Revelation 7:16-17 (NLT) So make every drop, word, and action count.

Scriptures to enjoy:

Genesis 1:2
John 4:13-14
Hebrews 10:22-23
Revelation 7:16-17

Prayer: Thank You, Jesus, that You will not only provide the water that we need but every other need we have in this life if we only trust in You and Your Salvation. Amen.

Love is Costly

It cost Jesus His life. He sacrificed it willingly all for me. It was personal; He knew it was for me. Many are those who have given their lives in the line of duty such as the Nine Eleven responders, our law enforcement officers or firemen, our military personnel on battlefields around the world in defense of our freedoms and the freedom of others. It may not have been because they knew for whom they were serving and dying, but they made the choice and the sacrifices.

As we remember on this Memorial Day those who have given their all to protect and defend us, let us not forget the One who gave His all that we might gain our all in Him.

Scriptures to enjoy:

Romans 12:1-3
Romans 8:34
Romans 5:6-11

Prayer: Thank You, Jesus, for Your great sacrifice for me. Thank You for the ones who have been willing to serve to protect and defend our nation. May we never forget all that it cost them and You to bring us this protection and grace. Amen.

Looking

Looking backwards what do I see?
All my sin and misery
Regrets and losses staring at me
As I tried to please those watching
To satisfy my pride.

Looking inward what do I see?
Scars and stains and
Wasted energies in failed actions
As I tried to please me.
No successes in that only shame and defeat.

Looking forward what do I see?
Service to Jesus since He set me free
As He leads me to time in the Word
And to bended knees with confessions of sins as they arise
Because now on Him I rely.

Looking upward what do I see?
A mansion in heaven awaiting me
No more pain and suffering, no more tears of loss
For now all my needs are met in the joy I've found
As Jesus only I live to please.

Looking outward what do I see?
Others suffering needlessly
Lost and alone without the love of the Lord.

People who need the Hand of the Savior but refuse to reach out
Trying to please the world which cannot be done.

Looking outward I'm praying they'll find the grace of the cross.
I'm praying they'll come to the place where hope abounds
So they too can find rest in the Risen One
Because there is no pleasing the world
And God blesses abundantly if we only believe in His Son.

Scriptures to enjoy:

Philippians 3:12-14
Revelation 21:3-4
Acts 2:33

Prayer: Lord, help me to show the love of Jesus so others will want to know Him too. In His Name. Amen.

Like the Dove

In the Biblical account of the flood when Noah took the animals into the ark there was a dove he sent out after the rains had stopped. When Noah released the dove it searched for land on which to rest. Finding none it returned to Noah. Like the dove searching for land we search in our lives for fulfillment. Sometimes we think we find it in success or wealth or power. But the contentment is short lived if it exists at all.

Like Noah reached his hand out to the dove, God reaches out to us. "Let him have all your worries and cares, for he is always thinking about you and watching everything that concerns you." 1 Peter 5:7 (TLB) The dove chose to rest on Noah's hand. Will you choose to rest in God's hands as He reaches out to give you rest and fulfillment? The choice is yours. How will you respond?

Scriptures to enjoy:

1 Peter 5:7
Genesis 8:1-12
Jeremiah 31:3
Lamentations 3:22-26

Prayer: Dear God, thank You for reaching out to me and rescuing me through the sacrifice of Christ. Help me to reach out to others with that Good News so they too may find rest in You. In Jesus' name. Amen.

Light Up Your World

The flashlight is a way to provide light in darkness. Its source of power is batteries. Its batteries can be recharged or replaced when weak. The light it produces points the path to help the walker avoid obstacles or pitfalls in the path when switched on. When there is other light as in sunshine or other illumination, the flashlight may become unnecessary. It can be switched on or off. Although even in other light sometimes the flashlight is helpful to shine in dark corners. When the flashlight is turned off or its batteries are dead it shines no light.

Christians are like a flashlight. They get their light from the Source of Light, Christ. When they are in the Word, praying, having fellowship with other believers they are able to be recharged and continue to shine. When they shine with the Light of Christ in them they avoid habitual sin in their lives and do not become stumbling blocks for others who come in contact with them.

If we fail to recharge our spiritual batteries by neglecting our prayers or scripture reading, or missing times of fellowship, our lights may become weaker. In this weakened state Christ cannot shine as brightly through us. Then not only does our pathway become more treacherous but we may lead others on the wrong road. We cannot be a light in a dark world unless we switch on Christ and let the Holy Spirit light the way.

Scripture says: "You're here to be light, bringing out the God-colors in the world. God is not a secret to be kept. We're going public with this, as public as a city on a hill. If I make you light-bearers, you don't think I'm going to hide you under a bucket, do you? I'm putting you on a light stand. Now that I've put you there on a hilltop, on a light stand—shine! Keep open house; be generous with your lives. By opening up to others, you'll prompt people to open up with God, this generous Father in heaven." Matthew 5:14-16 (MSG)

So Christian, turn on your light and light up your world. Shine on for Jesus because " You have turned on my light! The Lord my God has made my darkness turn to light." Psalm 18:28 (TLB)

Scriptures to enjoy:

Matthew 5:13-16
Acts 26:17-24
Psalm 18:1, 16, 25-32

Prayer: Thank You, Jesus, for lighting my way. May I shine always for You. In Your name I pray. Amen.

Jesus is Coming–Are You Ready for Him?

If you were having guests for dinner, you would make preparations for the meal to be shared. If a dignitary was coming to visit your house you would no doubt clean it up. If a special occasion was happening at a given date you would make the necessary arrangements for the date to be as special as possible. Jesus is coming. We don't know the exact date and time so how can we prepare for it?

Make each day the possible day of His return. That means to make every moment count in the preparation. Live the moment as if Jesus was to be there in the next because we are told in scripture to be ready. Love each other, provide for the needs of others, share what you have, speak well and above all share the Good News of salvation with everyone. As we are ushered in to eternity we don't want anyone to perish because we didn't share. So be ready, now, for Jesus is coming soon. Are you ready for Him?

Scriptures to enjoy:

Hebrews 10:35-39
Luke 12:32-40
1 Corinthians 15:50-58
Revelation 1:7

Prayer: Jesus, keep my heart ready for Your return. Help me to share the message of salvation with all I meet so that they too may be ready to meet You and share in Your presence for eternity.

It's Thursday

As I listened to the radio announcer say, "It's Thursday and the weekend's almost here," I had two thoughts. The first was how sad that we continue to look for "tomorrow" or something better, different, or more exciting than the moment we are in. The Lord made today and gave us this moment to live in so that we could bring glory to His name. How it must sadden Him that we are never satisfied with the blessings He has given us right now.

My second thought was longer in coming and was really an analogy. In our world today the time is far spent and Jesus is coming again soon. The end of this world is nearer today than it was yesterday. If today is "Thursday" we don't have much more time to spread the Good News of salvation. We don't have many days left in which to bring sinners repentance and new life in Christ. Our response to Jesus's free gift of salvation determines our eternal destiny. If we don't bring the Gospel to others who will? The time is now. We may not have another opportunity. What are you doing with your Thursday?

Scriptures to enjoy:

2 Corinthians 6:1-2
Romans 13:11-13
Hebrews 2:1-4

Prayer: Lord, don't let me waste the resources You provide to me nor fail to acknowledge the blessings You give me every moment of my life. In Jesus's precious name. Amen.

Indulgent Children

Why are we a child-dominated society? Why have we abdicated our parental authority to be in control of our families? Why are we over-indulgent with our children? Are we too tired to do what the Lord has commanded us to do, to teach our children to "fear the Lord" (Deuteronomy 4:10)? The results we see today in our violent, inattentive, self-centered, disrespectful children are what the Lord warns us will happen.

We have allowed Bible reading and prayer to be taken out of our schools but we took them out of our homes first. How many families do you know today that sit down together for meals and pray a blessing over the food they have been given? Does your family? Do you have a daily time of prayer and devotions for your families? Do you even go to church or Bible study? It's time we stopped blaming "society" or the schools or whomever we want to cast the blame on and accepted the fact that we ourselves are the responsible parties. We have forfeited our authority and allowed the "state" in whatever form it takes to become the parent. That order is disrupting our Christ-centered country and allowing the evil one to dominate our lives.

But take heart, Christ has overcome the world and with God all things are possible. There will be consequences but as we pray for the Holy Spirit to lead us to reclaim our children and the role we are to play in training them, God will prevail and He does win. We can be on His side, but we must take action now. Pray for His Guiding Hand in your life and in the lives of our children.

Scriptures to enjoy:

Deuteronomy 4:9-10
Deuteronomy 11:16-21
Isaiah 54:11-14
John 16:33
Matthew 17:20

Prayer: Oh, Jesus, help us to follow Your guidelines for raising our children and influencing those around us. I pray now that You will forgive us for our sins of neglect and self-centeredness and help us to go forward in You as we submit to the Holy Spirit's leading that we no longer sacrifice our children's lives to the evil one. Guide us, Lord. In Your Name. Amen.

Imagine

Think of the person you love above all else, more than you love any other person or thing in this life. Do you realize God loves you more than you love that person you're thinking about? Because of His great love for you and me He sent His one and only Son Jesus to die for our sins so that God Himself could have a relationship, fellowship, with each of us. Imagine that kind of love! This relationship with God is only possible if we respond to His offer of love by accepting Jesus' sacrifice on the cross for our sins. All we have to do is accept Him and repent of our sinfulness. Even if we refuse to do this God still loves us just the same, but He can't have the relationship He wants with us because our sin stands between us and Him. Only Jesus can bridge that gap. Have you accepted Jesus as your personal Savior? If not, you can do so right now by praying to Him and asking Him into your life, confessing your sin, and accepting the new life He wants to give you through Jesus. May God through His Holy Spirit reach out to you right now that you may be made brand new in Him.

Scriptures to enjoy:

John 3:16
2 Corinthians 5:17

Prayer: Jesus, thank You for Your sacrifice for my sake. Thank You for bridging the gap to the Father so that I can have a relationship with Him. Holy Spirit, lead me as I seek to follow God's will for my life. In Jesus' name I pray. Amen.

If Only…

Lord, if I could only touch the hem of your garment
My life would be changed forever.
I'd be made whole.

Lord, if I could only touch the hem of your garment
My path would be made straight
So I could follow you

Lord, if I could only touch the hem of your garment
Everyone who touches me
Would see You too.

Scriptures to enjoy:

Matthew 9:20-22
Matthew 5:14-16

Prayer: Thank You, Jesus, for showing me the way to live. Help my life to be a testimony of Your love for us all. Amen.

I Have Called You Friends

Can you imagine being a friend of Jesus? The Creator of the Universe calls me. And yet there is a scripture that says Jesus calls us friends. If scripture says it I believe it is true. What does it mean to be a friend? I spend time with my friends either in person or on the phone or by email or Facebook. I keep in touch; I share confidences and dreams. The closer the friend the more time I spend and the more I share.

My friendship with Jesus doesn't require an internet or phone connection. All I have to do is pray and He hears me. His words speak to me in the Bible. His Holy Spirit walks with me daily and shows me Jesus' plan for my life.

Who's your best friend? Jesus wants to be. You can become Jesus' friend by accepting His free gift of salvation right now. Invite Him to be your friend and He will never leave you nor forsake you.

Scriptures to enjoy:

John 15:13-15
Hebrews 13:5-6

Prayer: Dear Lord, thank You for my friends especially for the friendship You allow us to have with You. Help that relationship to grow daily and we fellowship with You. Amen.

I AM has sent me

All too often I make excuses like Moses did when commissioned by the Lord to go to Egypt and lead the Israelites out. It meant for Moses a confrontation with the pharaoh which was no doubt terrifying for him. Moses made excuses about why he couldn't possibly be the right choice and why he shouldn't go. But the Lord emphatically told Moses "I AM WHO I AM. Say this to the people of Israel: I AM has sent me to you." Exodus 3:14 (NLT)

Now I am not commissioned to go before a pharaoh or to lead the Israelites out of Egypt like Moses was but the Lord has given each of us a mission to accomplish during our lives on this earth. He also gifts us with what we need to perform the tasks presented to us. But we often get too busy in our own plans to heed the Lord's will or be bothered with doing what He wants us to do. In fact, sometimes we don't even acknowledge that the Lord has anything to do with our lives. As Christians we are called to do what the Lord sets before us.

Rather than become complacent in our Christian walk we need to say with Isaiah: "Here I am. Send me." Isaiah 6:8 (NLT) For like the great I AM sent Moses, the same I AM is sending us out daily. Go! Spread the Good News!

Scriptures to enjoy:

Exodus 3
Matthew 28:19-20

1 Corinthians 12:4-5
Isaiah 6:8

Prayer: Jesus, give me the courage of Isaiah to go out for You. Take away my excuses and make me useful to bring You glory. Amen.

How Much Faith Do You Have?

In John's gospel we have the first miracle Jesus performed during His earthly ministry. Jesus' mother Mary demonstrated her faith in His ability to correct a situation when the wedding they were attending ran out of wine. The servants pouring the wine had faith to do what Jesus told them to do when He said to fill the pots with water. Jesus provided what was needed to replenish the wine supply for the wedding. He provided it just at the moment it was needed. There was neither too little nor too much. But it was the best that could be given according to the review of the master of the wedding feast.

Do you have faith that Jesus can do what He says He will do? Jesus promises to meet our needs "And this same God who takes care of me will supply all your needs from his glorious riches, which have been given to us in Christ Jesus." Philippians 4:19 (NLT)

Do you trust the Lord to meet your every need, every day? Do you have enough faith? Do not be frightened like the disciples were but have faith in Jesus. "Then he asked them, "Why are you afraid? Do you still have no faith?"" Mark 4:40b (NLT)

Scriptures to enjoy:

John 2:1-12
Philippians 4:19
Mark 4:36-41

Prayer: Thank You, Lord, for always meeting my needs. Help me to trust You more. Amen.

How Much Do I Need Jesus?

I need Jesus for everything, for every breath I take. He gives me life. He provides for my basic physical needs in food to eat, water to drink and a house complete with my family to share it. Jesus provides me a constant Companion in the Holy Spirit. He is my personal Guide leading me through every day in every way. I need Jesus who provided me with salvation from my sins so my spiritual life could be restored to a right relationship with the Father. This gives me hope for my future. One day Jesus will have a place prepared for me in heaven where He will personally take me to that I may spend eternity with Him. My praise will join with the heavenly throng in praise forever, a joyous celebration never ending. Jesus is my Provider, Sustainer, Guide and Hope. Is He yours?

Scriptures to enjoy:

John 15:1-5
John 14:1-6
Zephaniah 3:17
1 Peter 1:3-5

Prayer: Jesus, I need You for everything. Let me never forget that without You I can do nothing. To You be all praise and glory. Amen.

Going Through the Motions

I was a public school teacher for many years. One year I wrote a dedication to a graduating class titled "Give It Your All." It was to be an encouragement to these graduates to embrace their futures whole-heartedly to pursue their dreams and goals with the zeal that make success most likely.

Isn't that what God wants of us. We are to pursue Him with our whole heart, nothing less. We are not to go through the motions of worship, Bible study, prayer, according to some preconceived plan we created. God has a plan for each of us that requires our attention to Him not to the things we think are important.

Matthew West sings a song on a Christian radio station I listen to. It is called "The Motions" that speaks to this issue. Some of the words include: "I don't wanna go through the motions

I don't wanna go one more day without Your all consuming passion inside of me I don't wanna spend my whole life asking what if I had given everything instead of going through the motions?"

So I challenge you like I did that graduating class to give it your all as you serve the Lord today rather than going through the motions. Let His word be your all consuming passion as you draw nearer to Him today.

Scriptures to enjoy:

1 Chronicles 29:11
Colossians 3:1-3, 23

Prayer: Dear Lord, help my activities be honestly for You not just going through routines that become complacent and meaningless. Help me to give my all to everything I do for it is done as unto You. In Jesus' Name. Amen.

God Planned for You

Think of all the planning that God had to do to create you and to bring you to where you are today. God arranged for your parents to meet, regardless of the circumstances of your birth God has granted you days of life experiences both the good and the bad to bring you into this day. No matter what you are facing at this moment in time God knows about it and has a plan for it to work for good if you are His follower. His plan is perfect.

If God orchestrated all of this from your creation to bring you to the here and now why do you find it so hard to trust Him to lead you through today?

Scriptures to enjoy:

Romans 8:28-29
Proverbs 3:5-6

Prayer: Dear God, help me to trust You in all things and to realize that You are involved in all the details of my life no matter what they are. Thank you. Amen.

God Fights for Us

In the Old Testament story of the rebuilding of the wall of Jerusalem in Nehemiah many factions tried to interrupt the successful complete of this task. Nehemiah armed his workers and, his job done, relied on God to fight the battles. He said, "...our God shall fight for us." Nehemiah 4:20 (KJV)

This reminds me of my Christian walk. There are temptations to stray from the path Jesus set before me. There are pressures to belong to the world and perform how the world performs. But if I will remember that Christ already won the war and I am armed with His power all I am required to do is rely on Him to fight each battle on my behalf. Then will my joy be overflowing.

Scriptures to enjoy:

Nehemiah 4:16-20
Ephesians 6:10-17

Prayer: Dear Lord, continue to remind me that You are in charge of my life. Thank You for winning my war. In Your Name. Amen.

Glorious Changes from Divine Grace

When Jesus comes into our lives He changes us into the new creations He wants us to be. This is a glorious change from the deadness of sin to the life we now have in Christ. This change is only because of Christ's love for us and the grace that came to us when He died in our place on the cross. This new life carries responsibilities for us. Paul says in the book of Ephesians that "we are God's masterpiece. He has created us anew in Christ Jesus, so we can do the good things he planned for us long ago." Ephesians 2:10 (NLT)

This means that we have a mission before us. Because God gives us good things to do we should be doing them daily. If we are standing still things aren't getting done. Standing still doesn't get us down the path God wants us to travel. If we are standing still something the Lord has planned for us to accomplish doesn't get done. A card doesn't get sent, a phone call isn't made, a neighbor isn't comforted, a message isn't delivered, the Good News isn't shared. Whatever the things planned for us we have a responsibility to carry them out. With the Lord's help through the power of the Holy Spirit living in us now we can perform whatever the Lord has for us to do.

Live in the newness of life in Christ. Enjoy the glorious changes He has made in you by His Divine Grace and get started on the path He has set before you. No more standing still.

Scriptures to enjoy:

Ephesians 2:1-10
2 Corinthians 5:17

Prayer: Thank You, Lord, for the glorious change in me. Help me to keep moving as I live the life You have set me on. In Jesus' name. Amen.

Getting to Heaven

There is A way to heaven. That way is to confess your sins and accept Jesus as your Savior and Lord. It is a narrow way and cannot be compromised. Scripture says: "Enter by the narrow gate; for wide is the gate and broad is the way that leads to destruction, and there are many who go in by it. Because narrow is the gate and difficult is the way which leads to life, and there are few who find it.." Matthew 7:13-14 (NKJV) Jesus is the ONLY way to heaven. There is no other way. We must acknowledge that we are sinners and that we need the Savior.

Once we make the commitment to follow Jesus He will make it possible for us to have the life He wants us to have on earth. As we prepare to go to heaven, as we depend on Him, He provides us rest from our struggles and freedom from our sin. "Are you tired? Worn out? Burned out on religion? Come to me. Get away with me and you'll recover your life. I'll show you how to take a real rest. Walk with me and work with me—watch how I do it. Learn the unforced rhythms of grace. I won't lay anything heavy or ill-fitting on you. Keep company with me and you'll learn to live freely and lightly." Matthew 11:28-30 (MSG)

Keep in mind that light is the burden of living a life for Christ, but narrow is the way to get to heaven. We must decide to accept Jesus as THE WAY.

Scriptures to enjoy:

Matthew 7:13-14
John 14:6
Matthew 11:28-30

Prayer: Dear Jesus, thank You for preparing a way to heaven for me. Help me to trust You to carry the burdens of my life as I learn to follow You. In the Name that is above all names, Jesus. Amen.

From Heaven to a Manger

From heaven to a hillside God sent His angels
Their message one of joy
Announcing Jesus' birth.

From the hillside to a stable
The Christ-child came to earth
His birth one of great joy to angels, shepherds, me.

From the manger to the Cross the Lord was made to trudge
To save the world from sin
His love reached down to me.

From the Cross to my heart the Christ, my Savior comes
My joy is made complete
As in my heart He lives.

Scriptures to enjoy:

Luke 2:1-20
Job 19:25
2 Corinthians 6:16

Prayer: Heavenly Father, thank You for sending us Jesus that we may live forever with You because of Him. Amen.

Foreign Language

Have you ever had a conversation with someone and felt you were speaking different languages? Either of you could get your point across to the other. So you tried a different approach and used more emphatic speech and so it went. And you went away, both disappointed and frustrated, feeling you'd lost somehow.

I wonder if that is how the Lord felt when the rich young ruler turned to leave. Perhaps he didn't understand, or maybe he did and didn't want to comply with what the Lord requested of him. In my life, how many times have I failed to comprehend what the Lord is showing ME in His Word or maybe I know what He is telling me and I just don't want to do it. So I turn away from the path the Lord wants me on and do things my own way ignoring the consequences.

Scripture is clear: "Therefore, to him who knows to do good and does not do *it,* to him it is sin." James 4:17 (KJV) So do not ignore what Jesus is calling you to do for "…with God everything is possible." Matthew 19:26b (TLB)

Scriptures to enjoy:

Matthew 19:16-26
James 4:17
Romans 7:14-15
Revelation 2:1-7

Prayer: Forgive me, Lord, for failing to understand Your messages, or ignoring them. Thank You for continuing with me even if we don't always seem to speak the same language. In Jesus' Name. Amen.

Foolish God

Often I am confused. I like to think that this confusion will pass and I will have some profound piece of wisdom to replace it and this will be a phenomenal revelation I can share with others. Unfortunately, I am frequently wrong in this thinking because my sense of dismay was over something so absurd as misplaced keys or poor scheduling that required me to be two places at once.

I am reminded in this scripture that God choses when things will occur. "But God chose the foolish things of the world to shame the wise; God chose the weak things of the world to shame the strong." 1 Corinthians 1:27 (NIV) If we want to be wise in the sight of the world we are often weak in the Lord. God is not foolish, I am when I think more of myself than of Christ and the example I am to be for Him in my activities.

Scriptures to enjoy:

1 Corinthians 1:25-31
Psalm 53:1

Prayer: Dear God, help me to put things of this earth in their proper place and to keep my eyes on You. In Jesus' Name. Amen.

Follow Me

If you have no problems (sufferings) you need to examine who Jesus is to you and what you are doing for Him. Just as Jesus called the disciples to follow Him, out of their careers, away from their familiar surroundings, He has called you and me to follow Him along the path He has chosen for each of us. The disciples suffered persecution and death in most cases for the sake of Christ. We may not be called to leave home and go to the mission fields to suffer persecution and death. We may not be imprisoned for sharing the Gospel. But scripture tells us we will face suffering if we accept Jesus as Savior and strive through His Holy Spirit to follow Him. Satan isn't willing for us to live for Christ. Satan wants us to continue in our sinful natures to reject the call of Christ.

The Lord promised us protection from the evil one. He promised to be with us and if the reward of salvation from our sins isn't enough we also receive a home in heaven with Jesus for eternity. Will you follow Jesus or will you follow the world? Are you afraid to share the Gospel and follow Jesus or are you willing to surrender to His call to "follow me?" "Then said Jesus unto his disciples, If any man will come after me, let him deny himself, and take up his cross, and follow me. For whosoever will save his life shall lose it: and whosoever will lose his life for my sake shall find it." Matthew 16:24-25 (KJV)

Scriptures to enjoy:

Philippians 2:1-18
Matthew 5:3-10

Matthew 16:23-25
1 Peter 3:14

Prayer: Thank You, God, for sending Jesus to be the Perfect Lamb that I might be saved from my sins and be forever in Your care. In His Name. Amen.

Fear of Failure

Fear of failure is all around.
Fear of failure looms very loud.
Fear of failure holds me down.
Fear of failure is not God's will.
Fear of failure is rolled away.
Fear of failure is gone today.
Because in the will of Christ I stand
It's all part of His perfect plan; nothing can take it away

So cast your fear of failure off to one side as in Him you too abide.
Never looking back but pressing on toward the promised prize.
His loving arms are open wide as on you he waits
That you might listen as to you He calls: "Come, follow me"
And in Me abide.

No more do I fear failure because in Christ I am secure.
Because my Lord is near, always here beside me as in Him I live and trust.
He is here to answer every plea where failure lurks.
But I no longer fear the failure as His promises are true.

He is always with me no matter where I go
So my life is in His hands, my future is all planned.
There is no longer fear of failure because He is my Lord
And everywhere that He leads me it is He that is at work.

Scriptures to enjoy:

Mark 1:16-18
John 14:16
John 15:4-10
Psalm 139:1-6

Prayer: Thank You, Jesus, that I can rest in You and You will always guide me as in You I live. Amen.

Eternity

Our responses to Christ give us direction for our lives. If we say yes to Jesus, accept Him as our Savior, our mission on this earth becomes one of serving Christ by serving others. Our eternity is sealed with Christ by this simple acceptance and when our lives on earth are completed we will go to the place Jesus has prepared for us in heaven. There is room for all. "In My Father's house are many mansions; if it were not so I would have told you. I go to prepare a place for you. And if I go and prepare a place for you, I will come again and receive you to Myself; that where I am, there you may be also." John 14:2-3 (NKJV)

If we reject Christ, turning our backs on His forgiveness, our direction becomes one of ego-satisfying attempts to fulfill our own desires. That never works because God created us to have fellowship with Him. But He will not force us to do so. Our rejection of Christ's salvation offer dooms us to an eternity separated from Him in hell.

The choice is ours to make. Time is very short. Paul says in 2 Corinthians 6:2b (NLT): "Indeed, the "right time" is now. Today is the day of salvation." What choice will you make? Your life for all eternity depends on it.

Scriptures to enjoy:

John 14:2-3
2 Corinthians 5:14-6:2

Prayer: Jesus, thank You for the free gift of salvation offered to all. Help many to accept it now. In Your Name, I pray. Amen.

Do Not Be Afraid

When Jesus comes to us are we afraid? He spoke the world into being, calmed the winds, healed the sick. His power is beyond anything we can comprehend. But He has told us not to be afraid. So why am I afraid? It is because in order to follow Jesus I must surrender my will to His. I must become less that He may become more. In this world today it makes me vulnerable and out of control. I may be ridiculed, scorned, criticized, and left out. Am I willing to do that? If I am not willing to surrender to Jesus' will I should be afraid. But if I do follow Him I have nothing to fear and I have His peace to surround me. Are you afraid of Jesus? Why not follow Him right now?

Scriptures to enjoy:

Matthew 14:27
John 16:33

Prayer: Lord, take away my fears as only You can. Use me for Your glory as I am available in my surrender to You. Thank you, Jesus. Amen.

Day by Day

The Lord didn't call us to climb every mountain or even to scale one mountain clear to the top in one day with one step. He did call us to take each step in Him, to be led by His Holy Spirit, all the way, day by day, every day. He is with us. Abide in Him and in His rest today as you take each step on the path you are going down as you are led by the Holy Spirit in your walk.

Scriptures to enjoy:

John 15:4-11
Matthew 11:28-30

Prayer: Lord, thank You for Your ever present love and guidance for me. Lead me every day in every way through the power of Your Holy Spirit, I pray. Amen.

Daily Grind

It seems like routines plague us. We get up, go to work or school, come home, go to bed then start all over. Oh, the problems of the day sometimes are different but much of the time they are the same too: issues with coworkers or children, financial stresses, not enough hours to do what we really want to do in the day.

Scripture tells us, "this is the day that the Lord has made. We will rejoice and be glad in it." Psalm 118:24 (NLT). So no matter what the rut you feel like you are in may be today is a new beginning. Remember that the Lord's mercies are new every day. It's like He continues to give us another chance. Rather than face the day as a boring routine, rejoice! The prophet Jeremiah reminds us that the Lord loves us and provides us new mercies daily. There is nothing boring about today. The Lord is with me and I will rejoice. How about you?

Scriptures to enjoy:

Psalm 118:14-24
Lamentations 3:22-25

Prayer: Lord, thank You that I can participate in today. Thank You that Your faithfulness to me is never ending. I praise You, Jesus. Amen.

Crucifixion or Resurrection

Too often we want to go straight to the resurrection and to skip the crucifixion and its pain. For Christ the suffering of the crucifixion was painful, shameful, humiliating and it ended in death. Christ's physical death, the death of separation from God due to the sins of man. God turned His back on His only Son that those sins might be forgiven and we might again be able to enjoy a relationship with the Father.

For us the crucifixion is a promise of redemption, salvation. To get to the Resurrection Christ suffered for me. For me to get to the resurrection to dwell with Him in heaven for eternity I too must be crucified. My self must die that I may live for Him and He in me.

The sin that separated me from God's fellowship has been forgiven with my acceptance of Jesus Christ as My Lord and Savior. My suffering in this life is temporary but my life in Christ is eternal.

The promise is mine and yours. The acceptance is a choice each makes. Will you crucify yourself to get to the Resurrection of life with Christ forever?

Scriptures to enjoy:

Isaiah 53:4-5
Isaiah 25:8
1 Corinthians 15:21
Revelation 21:4
2 Corinthians 5:17

Prayer: Lord Jesus, thank You for going to the cross and being crucified that You might conquer sin and death and be raised again so I can be saved. Amen

Crisis Time

I am continually reminded of the awesomeness of God through the ways in which He meets my needs. The Word says: "…they that seek the Lord shall not want any good thing." Psalm 34:10b (KJV)

I have begun to realize in my life that I become practically unteachable unless I am in a crisis situation. So God gives me one "crisis" after another in order to prove my dependence on Him and to improve my relationship with Him. If I become comfortable, I tend to become complacent toward God.

In order to be used of the Lord I must not be a lukewarm Christian, so the Lord allows challenges in my life that force me to grow. My prayer is that when I face, and with His help, handle these "crisis" situations others may see my faith and come to know Christ because of what they see of Him in me.

Scriptures to enjoy:

Psalm 34:10b
Psalm 37:4-8, 24-28
Revelation 3:16

Prayer: My Father, thank You for meeting my needs and leading me where You want me to go. Thank You for continuing Your work in me. In Jesus' Name. Amen.

Count the Cost

Have you ever started something, to prepare a meal, build a fence or shed, make an outfit, only to find you lacked the ingredients, tools or materials to complete it. So the project either lies unfinished or gets trashed. Sometimes we begin a new Bible study, devotional, or prayer series only to stop in the middle because it didn't meet our needs, took too much time from other activities, or interfered with something else we wanted to do.

Jesus warned us to be sure to count the cost, consider the commitment or obligation before we accept the call to follow Him. He wants us to know it won't be easy when we decide to become a Christian and walk with Him, but if we do make that decision, accept His salvation for our lives, the result with be worth the cost. We will have the Holy Spirit living in us as the guarantee for Christ in us and we will live with Him forever.

From the Word: "A large crowd was following Jesus. He turned around and said to them, "If you want to be my disciple,... So you cannot become my disciple without giving up everything you own."" Luke 14:25, 26a, 33 (NLT)

Scriptures to enjoy:

Proverbs 16:1-6
Psalm 37:3-7
Luke 14:28-30

Prayer: Lord, help me to be willing to serve You no matter what it costs me because You gave everything to provide me with eternal life. In Jesus' name. Amen.

Comfortable in Your Own Skin

Sometimes I wonder what others see when they look at me. Do they see a smile or a frown? Are they drawn to me because I seem inviting or are they pushed away because I appear unfriendly or hostile? How we are seen by others may have something to do with how we see ourselves. Do we concern ourselves with our outward appearance making sure our hair is combed or our shirt is tucked in? Or do we focus on our inward development? Are we prepared to meet others because we have spent time with the Lord before we go out? Are we allowing the Holy Spirit to guide us as we go about our daily activities?

The Word of God tells us that we are made in the image of God (Genesis 1:27). If God is satisfied with His creation and He is (Genesis 1:31), why are we dissatisfied with ourselves? We are to love others as we love ourselves (Mark 12:30-31). It would seem that we don't share God's love for others because we don't love ourselves. But if God made us and knows us, and scripture says this is true (Psalm 139:1-3), it seems to me I should be comfortable in my own skin. As long as I am walking with the Lord, growing in my relationship with Him, and loving others as He commands me, I should be satisfied with the one God has created me to be.

That doesn't mean I am perfect like God is. But it means I should not put myself down, nor should I do that to others. It means I need to seek the Lord first in all things so I'm sure I'm on the path He wants me on and not wandering off on my own. Don't buy into the lies of the world but focus on the Truth of the Word of God and be comfortable in your own skin—God didn't create you to be a critic but to love as He first loved you. You are special to Him.

"And whatsoever ye do in word or deed, do all in the name of the Lord Jesus, giving thanks to God and the Father by him." Colossians 3:17 (KJV)

Scriptures to enjoy:

Genesis 1:27-31
Mark 12:30-31
Psalm 139:1-6
Colossians 3:14-24

Prayer: Lord, help me to be comfortable with Your creation in me and to help others see their worth in You. In Jesus' name. Amen.

Cloudy or Clear, Jesus is Near

The clouds over the hills as viewed from my dining room window were black and ominous looking. They appeared dense and stormy. It looked as if we were in for rain. But as the morning moved forward the clouds brightened and lessened. The sun shone and we got no storm.

How often we view our days as those angry storm laden clouds. Our problems are too dense, too burdensome to be borne. We see no end in sight to the troubles we envision. But as we "cast our burdens on Him" the problems seem to lessen and fade. The storms are averted or at least become manageable because Jesus shoulders the load.

Scriptures to enjoy:

Philippians 4:6-9
1 Peter 5:7

Prayer: Thank You, Jesus, for being my constant Shelter even if storms do come and for taking my burdens as Your own. In the Name that is above every name, Jesus. Amen.

Christians, Stand Firm

Christians in America have been used to accepting the world's standards of behavior because for most of our history our moral structure was based on Judeo-Christian values. Because of our historical bias we are now astonished to find that things have changed for us. Where has this erosion come from and where did it start?

While the percentage of Americans claiming to be Christians has remained relatively unchanged for the last several decades, a majority of citizens somewhere around 85%, Christians are now confronted with being labeled intolerant or a terrorist threat because we do not accept the morality touted in current American media and the lifestyles of some. Although some changes have been subtle, like the changing vocabulary on prime time television, others have been more in-your-face demands, like marches on city streets or picketing of businesses that stand on Biblical principles.

Every major group in this country can claim legal protection against persecution except Christians. We are no longer free to practice truths we hold based on Biblical standards of behavior if they don't conform to what the new America finds acceptable. Businesses are shut down, Christians are fired from jobs, and children are suspended from schools for holding to the Name of Christ and living by the inerrant truths of God's word.

But Jesus warned us in scripture that we would not be accepted but rather would be persecuted. So we must remember that as great as America has been, it isn't our home and that we are only protected by the blood of Jesus and not by some governmental provision or legislative mandate. I stand on the Word of God and I know others do too. So Christians, stand firm on the Word of God and on the promises of Christ our Savior.

Scriptures to enjoy:

John 15:18-20
John 16:32-33
Ephesians 6:10-20

Prayer: Thank You, Jesus, for leading us daily as we trust in Your Word, which is Truth. Help us to be bold in the face of persecution and to stand firm for the beliefs we know are right. Amen.

Building Blocks

Children use different kinds of toys or other objects to create their buildings, cities or other structures. There are companies with lucrative businesses that produce blocks for various age groups and with varieties of complexity in their offerings. As I watched my grandsons make things from the blocks they now use I was reminded how much they've grown and developed in the things they create and how different they are from one another.

The growth and development of our spiritual lives depends on the blocks we have used. If our foundation's cornerstone isn't Christ the sides will erode and crumble. In other words we cannot create a solid spiritual life without a structure that is solid at the base. Like my grandsons' buildings, forts and cities that have become more elaborate as they have matured our faith should grow stronger as we mature in our walk with the Savior. This is only possible if we know Christ and accept Him as our foundational building block.

What are you using as building blocks? The ways of the world lead to destruction, misery and spiritual death and an eternity separated from God. The Word of God, fellowship of believers in praise and worship, daily prayers and devotional times lead us to grow in our walk with our Lord. How solid is your foundation? Are you growing in your relationship with the One you know as Lord?

Scriptures to enjoy:

Psalm 118:21-23
Matthew 21:42-43
Matthew 7:24-27

Prayer: Lord, I pray that there will be growth in my life that reflects the love I have for You. Thank You for creating for me a solid foundation in Christ. Amen.

Blanket of White

We were blessed with a lovely snow storm yesterday. As I looked out the window and saw the snow covered yard it appeared all white. As the temperature warmed, the snow began to melt. I could see through the snow to the rocks and grass that were under the blanket of white snow. I was reminded of the cover the Lord provides for me and you. There is a profound difference between the snow covering my yard and the cover of Jesus over us.

According to the Word in Revelation we are told that those who "are victorious will be clothed in white." Revelation 3:5 (NLT) Further that victory will not be taken and the white robe will not be removed from us unlike the snow that melted and revealed what lay beneath. Jesus has cast away all the debris from our lives and filled us with His Holy Spirit that we can be seen by God through the righteousness of Christ. (Romans 5:17)

To be covered by Jesus righteousness we must accept Him as Lord and Savior, give up our sin and follow Him. Then the blanket of His covering will never melt away. "For God has said, "I will never fail you. I will never abandon you." Hebrews 13:5b (NLT) Accept Him today.

Scriptures to enjoy:

Psalm 103:11-13
Isaiah 6:7b
Romans 5:16-18
Hebrews 13:5b

Prayer: Lord, thank You for the covering of Your righteousness over all who believe in You as Lord and Savior. Amen.

Be An Encourager

If you have ever been on a roller coaster you can appreciate the parallel between that ride and real life. There are high points and low points in both. There is a song our church choir sang that had a line "Would you welcome loving arms if you'd never shed a tear?" Comfort is appreciated only when we are sad. Both of these ideas remind me that we don't appreciate the good in our lives until we see the disappointments. In my life I have come to realize that I trust the Lord to lift me out of those troughs far more quickly than I offer to praise and thank Him for the peaks. It seems that I do not learn as quickly as Job to say, "The Lord gave and the Lord hath taken away. Blessed be the name of the Lord." Job 1:21b (KJV)

Once we have had experiences that are distressful and have recovered we are able to encourage others when they find themselves in those situations. We can rejoice with their joys and cry with their sadness. We can be the arms that lift them up as we share the love of the Lord, even as He has shared the Father's love with us.

Life will continue to be a roller coaster ride of sorts as we walk the path before us. But as we lean on the Lord for our strength and comfort in all circumstances we become examples for others to see Christ shining in us. Be an encourager to someone today as ". . . in everything (you) give thanks..." 1 Thessalonians 5:18a (KJV)

Scriptures to enjoy:

John 15:8-10
Job 1:1-21

1 Thessalonians 5:15-18
Hebrews 10:22-25

Prayer: Thank You, Lord, for the good times and the bad. Help me to remember that in all things You are my strength. May I be encouraging to others as I seek to demonstrate Your love in the midst of those I meet. In Jesus' name. Amen.

Battlefield Earth

I didn't realize that I was in the midst of a war before I came to a relationship with the Living Lord. As I have grown in that relationship and studied His Word I have come to see the battles I am personally fighting. Since my life isn't too much different than that of each of you I can safely say you too are in the war. If you don't know Jesus as your Savior, you may attribute the things you go through as fate or luck or destiny. The truth is that Jesus died for each of us and wants to claim us as His own. But Satan wants as many of us as possible to reject Christ and continue to live in sin. Satan knows his days are numbered and he will lose the final battle as Christ reclaims His own.

This revelation may not be as profound to you as it has been for me but let me share with you what I know. If we don't know Jesus as Lord, we go through the motions of our lives having good times, bad time, ordinary days and stress filled days and we go to sleep at night knowing tomorrow will be another day. If we have accepted Jesus as our Savior, our lives become a battleground. Scripture says in Ephesians 6:12 "For we are not fighting against flesh-and-blood enemies, but against evil rulers and authorities of the unseen world, against mighty powers in this dark world, and against evil spirits in the heavenly places." (NLT)

Satan doesn't want us to follow Jesus and lead godly lives that reflect the love we have found in that relationship with our Lord. Satan casts doubts in our minds or causes circumstances to be difficult. But by knowing that Jesus is able to Guide our days if we rely on the Helper we know as the Holy Spirit those trials that come our way are not insurmountable problems in our lives. Jesus promises "And I will pray the Father, and He will give you another Helper, that He may abide with you forever." John 14:16 (NKJV)

We can rejoice in the middle of the difficulties because no matter how the current circumstance plays out our eternity with Christ is assured. In this present darkness, Jesus is the Way (John 14:6) and His Word is a Light unto our paths (Psalm 119:105). Jesus provides the armor to protect us in this battle so we can walk with Him (Ephesians 6:10-18).

The battle will rage. Will you be on the winning side?

Scriptures to enjoy:

Revelation 20:10-15
Ephesians 6:10-18
John 14:16
John 14:1-6

Prayer: Lord, I don't want anyone to miss Your calling. Help all to accept You that eternity with You may be secure no matter what our lives on earth are like. Amen.

Baby

Dedicated to my grandson before his birth

A baby is a treasure, a little piece of heaven
Sent to us to love.
A baby brings us joy more than any kind of toy.
Rattle and bottles, diapers and pins
Now clutter every room and unhinge our ordered lives
As into them they come.
A baby takes the strings of our hearts and gives them a giant tug
Every time he smiles or cries,
And melts away all other things when he some need displays.
And when he brings us that special hug, he invades the spaces
Of even hardened hearts.
Sweet, tiny baby child, cradled in loving arms,
Nestled near those who in your life will guide you
Keeping you safe from every harm as along life's path you travel
Moving closer to heaven.
M ay you always hide
Close by the Savior's side as in His Will you stride.

Scriptures to enjoy:

Luke 1:41
Luke 2:12, 16
John 16:21

Prayer: Thank you, Lord, for the joy of children. Help us as we nurture
them and help them grow to know You and Your love for us all. Amen.

A Right Relationship

Jesus makes us right with God. When we are born again by accepting Jesus Christ as Lord and Savior, He makes us a new creation. Scripture says: "This means that anyone who belongs to Christ has become a new person. The old life is gone; a new life has begun!"2 Corinthians 5:17 (NLT) Why is this important?

Because we are all sinners in need of a Savior. We can never do enough, or give enough or try hard enough to rid ourselves of our sin. But Jesus can. He gave Himself as a perfect sacrifice on the cross and made it possible for us to be forgiven from our sins and restored to the relationship God intended for us to have with Him when He created us.

Jesus is THE way, the ONLY way to the Father. John's Gospel says it like this: "Jesus told him (Thomas), "I am the way, the truth, and the life. No one can come to the Father except through me." John 14:6 (NLT) By accepting Jesus as our Savior we no longer will be separated from the relationship with the Father that was designed for us. The Bible tells us "… that nothing can ever separate us from God's love. Neither death nor life, neither angels nor demons, neither our fears for today nor our worries about tomorrow—not even the powers of hell can separate us from God's love. No power in the sky above or in the earth below—indeed, nothing in all creation will ever be able to separate us from the love of God that is revealed in Christ Jesus our Lord." Romans 8:38-39 (NLT)

Make that choice today to accept Jesus as Lord and make your relationship with Him right. Nothing you can ever do will be as important as that decision is.

Scriptures to enjoy:

Galatians 6:15
Isaiah 43:18-19
John 14:6
Romans 8:38-39
Psalm 119:105
2 Corinthians 5:17

Prayer: Thank You, Jesus, for Your sacrifice for me. Thank You for creating a way for me to be reconciled to the Father that I may be in a right relationship with Him forever. Amen.

A New Song

Perhaps you can relate to the psalmist David when he said: "For troubles surround me—too many to count! My sins pile up so high I can't see my way out. They outnumber the hairs on my head. I have lost all courage. Please, Lord, rescue me! Come quickly, Lord, and help me." Psalm 40:12-13 (NLT) If you know the life of David you know he often cried out to the Lord, sometimes because he had done sinful, wrong things. In this passage of the psalm David knows enough to wait for the Lord's deliverance. Why? Because David had been in trouble before and the Lord had brought him safely through the trial.

In my life I have learned to rely on the Lord's deliverance in more than one circumstance. Unfortunately, I continue to make trouble for myself, getting into situations because I didn't first seek the Lord's direction or didn't wait for His timing and tried to do things on my own, in my own strength. But like David I can seek the Lord over and over again and I know He will meet my needs, forgive my sin, and give me a new song.

What about you? Are you getting into problem areas in your life because you've made wrong choices or bad decisions? Have you done whatever you wanted whenever you wanted to and the results were not what you wanted or expected? The Lord is near and just waiting for you to call out to Him to meet whatever your need is. It may not be the way you want things to go or even what you anticipate, but the Lord's Way is perfect and He will bring you a new song and a new attitude as you trust in Him.

"I waited patiently for the LORD to help me and he turned to me and heard my cry. He lifted me out of the pit of despair, out of the mud and the mire.

He set my feet on solid ground and steadied me as I walked along. He has given me a new song to sing, a hymn of praise to our God." Psalm 40:1-3a (NLT) Jesus said: "I have told you all this so that you will have peace of heart and mind. Here on earth you will have many trials and sorrows; but cheer up, for I have overcome the world." John 16:33 (TLB)

Scriptures to enjoy:

Psalm 40
John 16:33
Isaiah 55:5-9

Prayer: Lord God, thank You for meeting my needs and rescuing me from the pits whenever I get into them. In Jesus' name. Amen.

About the Author

The author is a Christ follower who wants others to share eternity with the Lord Jesus in heaven. To that end she has written devotionals and shared with others what Jesus means to her..

The author has been involved in her local churches wherever she has lived. With a bachelor of arts degree in history and a master's degree in education the author was involved in curriculum writing throughout her 41-year career as a high school teacher. She was a public high school teacher for 35 years in California then moved to Idaho to teach junior and senior high school students at a private Christian school. Retired from classroom teaching the author now enjoys Bible study groups in the community and her local church both as a teacher and as a learner.

The author has two grown sons and three grandsons. She currently lives on the family farm in Idaho. She is enjoys traveling the country visiting family or historical sites. When she is not writing she enjoys quilting, reading, and studying the scriptures for deeper insights into the Word of God.

Printed in the United States
By Bookmasters